AF614436

ISBN 978-1-105-57455-9

In Memory of Bill Lisch

How Do You Pronounce Cadiz?

By

Wanda Wilferd Lisch

In the more than 25 years that I've worked at the Cadiz-Trigg County Tourist Information Center, I have heard many stories. Some have been funny, others informative, while others have been sad or even heart breaking. As I have repeated some of these stories to friends, many have suggested that I put these into a book.

It is not my intention to show how people are different or how alike we are. This is just a partial record of people that have crossed my path over the years. I have met a variety of people from all over the United States and Europe. A lot of Canadians have stopped in and I have met people from Australia, New Zealand, India and Africa. We all are individuals. Usually, if you treat them with respect, they act in kind. A few are angry or tired but with very few exceptions, they leave in a better mood.

I have worked longer than anyone at the Cadiz-Trigg County Tourist Information Center, in Cadiz, Kentucky. I order local brochures, keep the racks restocked and try to keep the Tourist Center clean. I also work with the lady that comes every two years and sells ads for our local Trigg County map. Our phone is made available to people who need their calls returned due to car problems or other emergencies. We also supply electricity for oxygen hook ups. I have also supplied coat hangers to people to open their locked cars. I welcome the people coming in the door like you would a visitor to your home.

The information center where I worked.

The Tourist Center has always been a popular place to meet. It is easy to find, and people from out of state can call local people they are visiting or I can give them a map and directions to their house.

Some people are in a hurry – you meet their needs and send them on their way. Others want to relax and rest and most really like to talk. They like to compare places that we both have visited. They talk about problems with their spouses or children; about a book they are writing. You just go along with what they seem to want since you may be the only Kentuckian they meet or especially a Trigg "Countian". It makes them want to come back for a longer visit. I have worn many hats.

I have been asked all kinds of questions, like what this is and that, growing along the roadside. Where are the horses? Where is the tobacco and why is that barn smoking? Is it on fire? (Usually, when they see smoke coming from a barn, it is the curing of tobacco that they are seeing) Some wonder why our corn is so short (it's just the particular variety of corn that is grown here) or where they can get good barbeque. Some need information on doctors, drug stores, veterinarians, and even nude camping!

I tell them that Cadiz is a unique little town with a lot of pride in the way its buildings, homes and yards are kept. I mention the antiques, local crafts, the ham festival and why we have the pig statues.

A Ham Festival pig statue.

I have had divorced parents, or their grandparents and other relatives meeting to exchange the children. I have seen the kids grow-up over the years. Real Estate people have met clients there. People meet to play golf, or to change clothes for various reasons. Sometimes to dress for funerals or the military personnel would want to change into casual clothes. People like to rest after driving for hours. They like to find a new place to vacation or plan a family reunion. They need information about how far down the road a place is, or how to get back on the right road. Some people are just hopelessly lost.

People will say, "I bet you have never been asked this question before"? I have been, usually several times, but only once about nude camping.

The most asked question has been, "How do you pronounce "Ca-dees"?" The road missed by the most travelers has been the West Kentucky Parkway at Exit 42. Some were surprised or annoyed at all of the 'dry' counties (no alcohol sales allowed) around the Lake. One fellow from New York did not even know what that meant. Since that time the laws have changed and Trigg County is no longer 'dry'. The most asked restaurant question before we got one - what exit is the next Cracker Barrel. We get all kinds of questions about the Kentucky Dam. The history of the Land between the Lakes National Recreation Area is very interesting to many. Of course we have questions about crafts, antiques, places to stay, where to eat and things for children to do.

I was blessed with a loving family and have no bad feelings or experiences from my childhood. Of course there were a few things I wish had been different. That would have changed the course of my life. I feel very personal about the song we sing in church "I Have Been Given Much I Too Must Give".

Me and my children, Eddie and Michele, in Hawaii.

Of all the blessings I have thanked God for; I have thanked Him most often for my two children, Glenn Edward, born January 1960, and Chris Michele, born January 1969. They were both beautiful babies, healthy and intelligent. I was always proud of them. I enjoy my son with his dry wit and outgoing personality. My daughter, with those big brown eyes, curls and a dimple made it very difficult to punish her when she did her antics.

Michele playing in the biscuit dough.

For example, at age two, when I told Michele to sit in her rocking chair and watch "I Love Lucy" while I vacuumed upstairs. When I checked on her she was sitting in her little chair watching TV with her feet up to her ankles in my canister of flour. Her grandmother had visited and had let her play in the flour around the edges of the counter while she made biscuits. Michele must have enjoyed the way the flour felt. I enjoy being with them as adults and with their children. I am more thankful now for my experiences, travels and the things I have, which happens, as we grow older. I was blessed with the family I was born into.

My mother, Pauline, was a single mom for several years. She and my dad, Wellman (Dickie) Wilferd, divorced when I was about 4 years old. We lived with her parents, Albert and Alice Puckett in Kuttawa and later in Golden Pond, KY. They were wonderful grandparents to me. It was a fun experience moving to the farm, riding in a wagon and getting a puppy for the first time when I was 6 years old. Being the only grandchild for years, I got a lot of love and attention and was maybe just a little spoiled. I don't think so.

When my mother was 29 years old she married Bill Carrigan. Along with a step-father I also got that little brother that I had always wanted. Ray Carrigan is 4 years younger than I am. We were 9 and 5, respectively, when our parents married. We lived in Paducah for about three years and in Detroit, MI for almost two years. The big city life was not for us, so we went back to Golden Pond until Ray and I graduated from Trigg County High School in Cadiz.

My mother's sister was a big part of my life. Mildred, or Mimmie, as all the kids called her, loved to spoil other people's children. Since she had no children of her own, my mother shared me with her. That later came to include Ray, our spouses and our children. When she and her husband, Porter Rogers, moved to Princeton, KY, my mother and I would often ride the train from Kuttawa to Princeton. I would stay for a week or two at a time. Mimmie would take me to the movies, taught me how to embroider and taught me songs like "Mairzy Doats". I so enjoyed sleeping under her Dutch Doll and Butterfly quilts. We lived next door to each other in Paducah and later lived in Detroit at the same time and again in Cadiz when Mimmie was married to Andrew Calhoun. She always loved to cook for the family, made great varieties of candy and always answered the phone with a cheery "hello".

My aunt, Mildred "Mimmie" Rogers.

I always enjoyed visiting both sets of grandparents. My dad's parents, Otto and Julia Wilferd, lived in Kuttawa and later in Harrisburg, Illinois. In my bathroom I have a small, green, frog planter. In the summer it was always on the front porch of my Wilferd grandparents' house with a plant in it. For whatever reason, my grandfather's nickname was "Toad". So, of course, I, as a child, named the planter frog "Otto". I cherish my little "Otto the frog". We had many laughs over "Otto" when I visited my grandparents in Kuttawa.

Many times, after a divorce, relatives don't make an effort to keep in touch with the children. That certainly was not the case in my family. My dad's two younger brothers always wrote, called and visited.

So many people's dream is to retire on the Lake - at least to be able to see the water from the deck. My uncle Jack had a dry wit; sometimes I think my son's sense of humor comes from Jack and also his brother, Bob, my dad's second brother. Jack moved to Lyon County, where he grew up, after retiring from the Navy and living in Iowa and Arizona. The real estate person was trying to sell him on buying on the water. Jack said, "After 30 years in the Navy, I don't care if I ever see the water again!" Bob's saying was, "I rest my case" after proving a point. He taught English and Journalism in a High School in Northern Illinois. His students really enjoyed his teaching and thought well of him. He was a widower so they took him out to dinner on his birthday.

Jack retired from the Navy and both he and Bob invested in real estate. Bob had wanted to be a doctor as his grandfather was. His sister had been a nurse. But, that would have taken too much money and too many years of schooling.

My dad, Dickie, and me in Indianapolis.

After serving in the Army during WWII my dad lived in Indianapolis, IN until his death. He would pick me up and we would visit his parents in Kuttawa a couple of times a year. I would visit with him in the summertime. He always dressed well and was movie-star handsome.

I'm sure that I am like many in that I thought my family was the best! My maternal grandmother, my Aunt

Mildred, my mother and I had the best times having lunch, out shopping or just visiting with each other.

A good friend in his early 90's asked me recently if I realized how much water has been inimical in my life. He has been my teacher in high school, performed the wedding ceremony for my first marriage, and has been my pastor in two different churches. After looking up the word 'inimical' I found it to mean hostile, unfavorable, adverse, unfriendly, and like an enemy. Both sides of my family had to relocate out of Kuttawa and Golden Pond due to the flooding of Lake Barkley. I was caught in a rip current in Hawaii while playing in the waves with my 10 year old son. I've had flooding in my house repeatedly, due to leaking water lines, roof leaks (both before and after having a new roof installed), and a poorly designed patio. I had never thought about it, but he seems to be right.

I have been working at the Tourist Center for over 25 years. I'm writing about this time in my life as I meet people from different areas and in different stages of their lives as they stop at the Tourist Center. As they share experiences and memories, it brings back memories in my life of other times and places I have lived and trips I have taken.

I have met a variety of people who have touched my life and shared parts of their life with me as they pass through the doors of the Tourist Center. So many people briefly touch your life; others for a day, a week, or a lifetime. Something about them lingers with you, with a word or smile or it may be just a feeling you get of joy, sadness or a longing for something. I always say every person has a book in them. A person's childhood and school years holds so many conflicting memories. The influence of your family, friends, neighbors and teachers makes the list endless. Your early adulthood, a job, marriage, raising children, the ups and downs in your personal life can influence your spiritual life. A death in the family, a divorce or un-expectant pregnancy can change the way you think or sometimes change the road you take as you travel the many lanes and highways in a lifetime.

Wanda and her mother, Pauline.

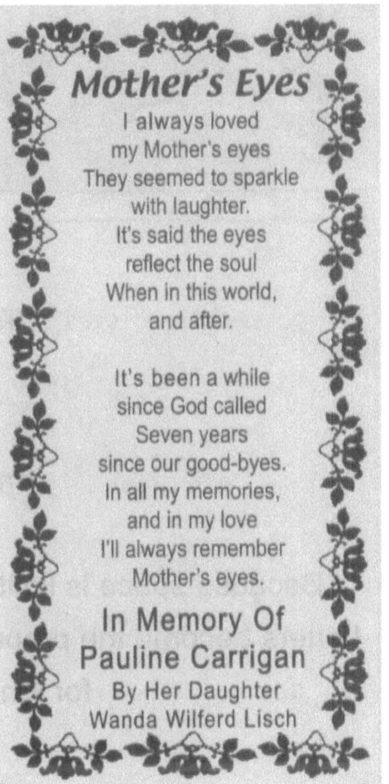

Mother's Eyes

I always loved
my Mother's eyes
They seemed to sparkle
with laughter.
It's said the eyes
reflect the soul
When in this world,
and after.

It's been a while
since God called
Seven years
since our good-byes.
In all my memories,
and in my love
I'll always remember
Mother's eyes.

In Memory Of
Pauline Carrigan
By Her Daughter
Wanda Wilferd Lisch

My mother's parents, Albert and Alice Puckett.

My father's dad, Otto Wilferd.

My grandmothers, Alice Puckett and Julia Wilferd.

Four generations: Lizzie, Alice, Pauline and Wanda, at the house on the hill.

Dedication

This book is dedicated to the memory of my husband, Bill Lisch. He was going to add "a little bull" to my facts to spice this book up a bit. He was a sounding board and critic, also an enduring and loving supporter. Bill enjoyed life more than anyone else I know. He gave so much and expected so little in return, just love.

Boating and fishing were high on Bill's fun to do list. We enriched our lives by traveling all the states, we had fun being with friends and Bill certainly enjoyed his Sunday school class and Tuesday morning men's bible study. He had the cutest dance step that we added to, and made our own unique way of dancing.

Bill was a gifted handyman. He could fix anything from woodworking to electrical wiring to plumbing. He was proud to have served in the US Navy and flew the American Flag every day, even before 9-11. He was in the American Legion and participated in all their military funerals, parades and other activities.

Bill in his American Legion uniform.

Bill drowned while swimming for our pontoon boat that had broken away from the dock. This was on August 13, 2008, the day after my birthday. He was a "young 74" in looks and action. I would never have written an ending to his life like that. A sudden loss is really a shock with no time to prepare your head as in an illness. Then, as in all deaths, you have to prepare your heart for the loss, the missing and the loneliness. Our 24 years and 4 months together were filled with laughter, travel and fun times with family, and certainly love and respect.

About a month after Bill died a lady stopped in the Tourist Center. She was originally from Kansas, and then lived in New Jersey. She has been living in Lyon County for several years. Her husband died in the 1990's. She said something profound as she was leaving. She said "We get a script that we did not write". How true that is. Working and sharing stories about our husbands' deaths with other women helped me in starting the healing process.

I often listen to women's health symptoms or complaints; sometimes we compare our problems; especially if their husbands have died. After Bill died I learned from others how to cope and handle things alone.

Wanda and Bill boarding the cruise ship, *Veendam*, bound for Alaska.

Wanda and Bill Lisch.

My son, Eddie, and me.

My daughter, Michele, and me.

My son, Eddie and his wife, Lee, son Eddie and daughters, Kelly and Jennifer.

My daughter, Michele and her husband, Dickie, and daughters Lindsey and Sierra.

My granddaughter, Sierra.

My granddaughter, Lindsey.

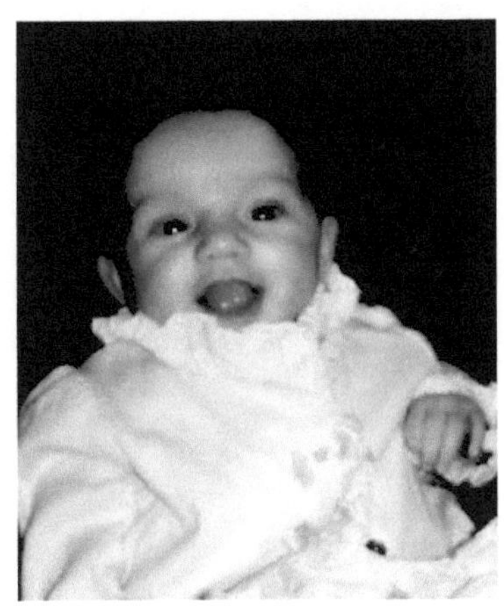

My great-granddaughter, Aubrey.

My grandson, Eddie and great-grandsons
Michael and Eddie IV.

My granddaughter, Jennifer.

My granddaughter, Kelly.

Around the World

I enjoy talking with people from all over the States and Internationally from most countries. The Canadians are so polite. Most people are very nice. I feel blessed to have met so many different people. A fairly young couple from Switzerland made such a positive impression. His lifelong dream was to drive across the United States. When I met them, they were headed to St. Louis on the way to California.

When people come in from Europe, it opens a flood of memories. Most people speak English pretty well. Usually if it is a couple, the man is more fluent in English. We talk of the 3 years I spent in Italy and the difference in the money now and other changes. I think about driving along the countryside by myself to a village where bolts of wool knit were on shelves. You take a picture of what you want and after picking out your color, they measure you and you go back in a couple weeks and pick-up a fully lined beautiful suit. There was a village where you would go that had huge blocks of cheese. They would give samples, and you would choose what kind to buy.

Wanda and the Oldsmobile before going to Italy.

One very nice Italian couple and I talked about Marastica. It's a town in Italy that had human chess games in the village, below a very nice restaurant. The restaurant set upon a mountain and the road was extremely narrow and winding. In our American Oldsmobile we would have to back up a little to make a turn. It was quite scary. It was a gorgeous Oldsmobile that I absolutely loved. It was silver with leather bucket seats. It was the kind of car you see in magazines with a couple in the moonlight dressed in formal attire. But while beautiful to look at it was not very practical for the narrow roads of Italy. To get into the courtyard of the restaurant you would have to back up a little to make a sharp turn to get through the iron archway.

When the Officers stationed in Germany had meetings with our Military Intelligence husbands; the wives were always eager to come to Italy. The Marastica was always a favorite place to have dinner and a trip to Venice to shop was always a must. I learned to snow ski and took many trips with the Wives Club. Our family enjoyed traveling in Europe, and we always had holiday meals with friends. My in-laws enjoyed Rome, the Leaning Tower of Pisa and Germany. I preferred Herculaneum to Pompeii; both had been buried cities near Naples.

A couple from Germany, who needed help, was trying to get to Chicago and could not speak English. He wanted to go 24 to 57, which I prefer. She thought by looking at the map, it would be better to go through Indiana. With no English spoken I thought Highway 41 through Evansville would be more difficult. I even pulled out some Italian language I remembered from living in Italy, which was no help. At times it can get you flustered!

I have met several couples from England on a holiday to America. My family's surname was Wilford which is English, and my great-grandfather, Dr. Wilford, originally from Mayfield, KY, changed it to Wilferd. I always thought it would be nice to take a trip there. I would like to drive along the pretty countryside and also see London. The tourists fly into different parts of the United States. Some have families that live in the United States. They return home to work and save their money, so they can return for another holiday. They rent a car and with each visit see different states. I enjoy their accent. One couple from Northern England was seeing Tennessee and Kentucky on a motorcycle. A music planned trip had fallen thru, so they were on their own. They were most enjoyable to talk with. Among the sites they visited were Chattanooga, Gatlinburg Area, Mammoth Cave and Renfro Valley.

In August of 2008 a nice couple stopped in. They were in their late 40s early 50's. She was from Iowa and later Chicago. He was from England. He has been in America 11 years; Kentucky is his 30th State to visit. Her daughter was in New Orleans during Katrina, but escaped to Chicago she said. He had made several trips to the U.S. over the years, but now they have decided to move to New Orleans.

An interesting group from Queensland, Australia visited. I saw 4 of the 5 people the young lady said were in her group of missionaries. They were a band. She wore a low riding short skirt with a top that showed a lot of stomach. I saw an older man and two younger guys. She talked about how prominent snakes are there. The snakes would go right through your home if you left your doors open; mostly poisonous ones. That changed my mind about visiting! Yet, others have visited and not seen any snakes.

An interesting couple visited quite a while telling about all the places they had lived. They were probably in their 60s. He was originally from Australia, she was from England and they met in Canada. They talked about living in Michigan, Australia, several other places on our map and are now in California. They apparently have adapted well to living in various surroundings.

I had quite a different conversation one day. This fellow's family were Jewish and originally from Russia. His mother was one of ten children and his dad was one of eight. Only he and his mother escaped during World War II, to Israel. No aunts, uncles or cousins made it out of

Russia. He enjoys traveling. He has been to Australia and New Zealand, but drew a map of Israel on our sign in sheet, where you would normally put the number in your party. He also drew it on a sheet of paper for me.

Two men from Mayfield all Mexicans brought a guy in that had a bus ticket to Mexico, but he spoke no English. They wanted to know where he could catch a bus. Upon checking we found out that a van would pick him up at McDonalds and take him to a bus station. There may be one at Fort Campbell, I think Clarksville and Paducah, but I don't believe Hopkinsville has a bus station any more. One of the fellows could speak English; sometimes it is a little difficult to communicate.

When people are visiting from the Baltimore, Maryland area, I remember the restaurant that we used to go to, around 1970. There were always long lines outside waiting to get in. It was called *Houstrum*. It was a beautiful place to eat, and it had lots of nice paintings on the walls. 20 years later Bill and I visited friends in Baltimore and enjoyed what had been done to the waterfront.

Several people over the years have either lived in or visited Hawaii. Since we had lived there for a time ourselves, there is a lot to talk about comparing all these things to do on the island. One couple, who was visiting us, was almost late getting to the airport because she did not want to leave the beach. The 2½ years we lived there were fun times.

Wanda visiting Kauai.

We lived on Oahu and visited Kauai and Hawaii, which they call the Big Island. I took hula lessons and we went to see Don Ho. We had more company there than anywhere we lived. Who would not want to visit Hawaii? I loved walking on the sand, riding the waves in with my son and playing with my daughter, even during the Christmas season! Lying on the mat near the beautiful palm trees with cool breezes and listening to the waves cresting was so relaxing. There were so many places to take our visitors; the Polynesian Cultural Center and Paradise Park to name a couple. After dinner, moonlit strolls on the beach imagining the stories or lives of the people sitting on the balconies on the hotels. Half an hour could be spent reminiscing with people about their visit in Hawaii. I went to see Elvis Presley perform and my son really enjoyed meeting Jim Nabors, "Gomer Pyle", at the airport.

Eddie and Michele on the beach in Oahu.

Over the years I have appreciated the couples from Canada. They are so polite and well-mannered. I had been in Canada only across from Detroit, New York and in Vancouver, and so it is always a pleasure to talk with Canadians about their country. Someone from Canada once told me how surprised she was when she and her daughter visited Paris. She thought the Eiffel Tower would be taller.

That same fall in 2009 a fellow, between the ages of 35 and 45, spent a lot of time telling me about Canada. I've been to towns in Canada three times. We discussed my visits from New York to Niagara Falls and how beautiful Vancouver was. I was very interested in learning more and he was very interesting. He was a Canadian Mountie, and he worked with computers. He was on the way to Atlanta to meet a girl who was a good friend. They were going to attend a rock concert before she went to

Europe. Their paper money is different colors. 20's are green and 10's are red, etc..... One and 2 dollars are coins. We discussed the difference between US and Canada; politics, health care and so forth. He said there were no dry counties that he knew of. Now there has been discussion about our paper dollars being replaced with coins.

One day six people on motorcycles from Alberta Canada were very interesting to talk with. They flew their bikes and themselves into Nashville. They were just 'tooling around' seeing the sights. This was in April of 2008 and the weather was nice.

A young couple from France stopped by, they weren't married but traveling together for a while in America; eventually they would be going their separate ways visiting different places and seeing friends.

An interesting couple was in the tourist center today. They are living on a farm in Tennessee that their son owns. They are more than ready to move as they usually live further west. They very much enjoyed visiting their son and family in South Africa. In fact, they loved it. Their son is a chiropractor and was teaching at a university. His wife is a veterinarian, and their children were young when they lived there. She said the people were nice, there were big malls; they went to several different towns. When they rode in a land rover or land cruiser during the first time they visited, a bull elephant came right up to them and sniffed them with his trunk. The son and wife are now in Australia. He is now head of the Chiropractic Department at the university. His wife also teaches there. Their granddaughter married an "aussie", but she wanted her wedding in South Africa at a game reserve. There are wild animals in their wedding pictures; including a giraffe standing between but behind them. She said they didn't see any snakes in Australia when I questioned them. Their grandson is in college in the United States. They were on their way to visit their other son in Wisconsin. As a young girl she had told her mother she was going around the world. She has done so twice even if most of it was spent flying over it.

I met an interesting woman age 86. She was driving from North Carolina to Vancouver, British Columbia. She had been visiting her son and his family but said that she couldn't live with her daughter-in-law more than three days, because like fish, she began to smell after three days. So she bought a house near them. Her son is her only child, and she has three grandsons. It's a 4000 mile drive from Vancouver to North Carolina, so she usually flies 3 to 4 times a year. She moved back to Canada after her husband died in 2000. She lived in Los Angeles most of her married life. She was curious about everything from what type crops were growing, to trees and everything on the highway. She owns 3 houses. The one in North Carolina and two in Canada, I'm sure money is no problem for her.

A family from Poland came in the tourist center. A man, his wife, daughter and father were with him. His father lived in Chicago and the man teaches English in Poland. He had taught English in the United States but says that his wife is the reason he's back in Poland. The wife and daughter spoke some English but with an accent. Both of the men spoke English well.

A family from Cadiz came in, she was originally from France, and he from South America. They met when they moved to Chicago. He ran a little restaurant that was a teenage hang out. They met, married and had a family. One year they went to Southern Illinois on vacation. Later they started vacationing at the Land between the Lakes National Recreation Area for several years with the children. They never thought they would move here. They came in to get Information on day trips for her sister visiting from France. She and her husband live on a tiny island off the coast of France; her husband is a fisherman. She still really has an accent.

It was interesting talking to the 2 American men, father and son, who have worked in Cadiz, Spain for years. They sent me several brochures from there. That Cadiz is pronounced differently than our Cadiz is!

Lost

There are also the difficult ones. Two women on their way home to Illinois, wanted me to find something for them to do in this area. They had come from Nashville and insisted there was nothing to do there. I informed them of some of the things we had enjoyed in Nashville. I also told them about this area. The same day a family was going to Bowling Green before the 4-lane, from Cadiz was completed; they only drove on 4-laned highways. So they insisted on going to Nashville, TN and taking Highway 65 back to Bowling Green, KY. I told them they could be in Bowling Green by the time they got to Nashville. You give them what they want, it takes all kinds.

One challenge was a woman on a bicycle. Her goal was to get out of Kentucky. She had a jacket on with several pockets full of candy and cans of drinks. She was angry and used several curse words. I told I would be glad to show her how to get out of Kentucky. I then proceeded to show her a map with different roads to take. Even she calmed down and acted nicer as she left.

One middle aged man was very irate as he entered the building. I'm sure that having to ask a woman for directions did not help any. He said he had driven all over the United States and had never been lost until the West Kentucky Parkway. I told him he was very fortunate to drive all over the United States and not once miss his road.

My husband and I have driven all over the United States, and almost every trip we take somewhere along the way we miss a turn or take a wrong road. In Salt Lake City, we had to ask several times how to get out to the Big Salt Mounds. One man wanted to send us over to Las

Vegas. I told him we did not want to gamble, we wanted to see the salt.

The Western Kentucky Parkway, coming from Paducah was missed so many times each month that we had a paper on our desk that people signed. They thought there needed to be more “signage” before the Eddyville area. Now people coming from the lakes looking for State Route 274 will end up here asking what happened to it. They take the bypass around Cadiz not knowing you need to take Business Route 68 in order to get to the 274.

An older couple from Georgia was going to Ohio. Neither could read a map. They wanted me to write down all the turns; exactly how and when to turn right or left to get them to the town they were going to in Ohio.

One frustration I haven’t forgotten. A fairly young fellow was trying to get to Louisville. I gave directions twice. I went over the map twice and told him twice, “Do not get back on I-24”. I watched as he left and promptly turned east onto I-24 going toward Tennessee.

Help

There are medical problems – while some need a hospital others need a physician or dentist and others just a drug store. The need for a veterinarian and lost animals are among problems presented to me. I have called on many resources. My Pastor and Pastors of other churches, the police, my husband, helping hands, and I make numerous phone calls to get that information they need.

Another time a gentleman left cards for me to mail for him at the post office. It was a simple thing for me to do but was out of the way for him. He wrote: Your attendant is great.

People are so appreciative of small favors when they are traveling. They write nice compliments on sign in sheets. Several times I have mailed cards, letters and even bills. I once mailed a key back to an apartment.

A very upset couple, especially the woman, was here in July of 2004. They had been traveling with two cats. They had lost a black longhaired cat early Wednesday morning. She said they had made a couple of stops before they realized in St. Louis that only one cat was in the back of the van. They were here Wednesday afternoon. They had returned to both places they had previously stopped, calling for, and searching for, the cat whose front paws were declawed. They called back on Thursday, very concerned, and left a number to call if she is seen. They would drive back from Kansas to retrieve her if found. Think the cat found its way home?

Joseph P. had been with a woman in North Carolina for 7 years when she kicked him out for another man. He had owned four dogs but only left with one. This was his story: "He picked up a hitchhiker, and had his money in an envelope on the dashboard and the hitch hiker stole it." He wanted to work, so I let him pull weeds in our flower bed for $10.00. I made several calls but couldn't find him work. I got him a meal from Cadiz Restaurant, through the Ministerial Association of Cadiz by calling the Methodist Church, as I have done on other occasions. I'm proud that Cadiz can be a caring and giving community.

A lady called from her home in Nashville, Tennessee. It was about 9:30. She thought she'd left her billfold next door at the service station, and asked if I'd go next door and check for her. I went over and yes, they had it locked up. We both felt relieved. She could pick it up. When I told her this, she wanted me to send it to her. She would tell them over the phone what was inside of it, identifying all of the contents and telling them her social security number as well as the amount of money left in it. They would not release it to me, only to her. After hearing this, she wanted me to call the police- which I did. The officer came out and said the same thing because of the fact that there is too much fraud and identity theft. He called her and explained, but we did give her the main office's number in Hopkinsville. That incident really took up a lot of my morning. On this job, as I have said before, you wear many hats.

Just today a little older fellow coming from Maine, going to Missouri, was completely out of gas and money. It was April 28th; he would have no money until after the 1st of the month. He wanted $20 of gas to get his old motor home to Paducah. He had spent all his money on parts. I called the Methodist Church, and then the Minister called over to the Shell service station to approve the gas. The fellow walked over with a can to get enough in his motor home to drive to the service station and finish up the $20.00. Other times the Ministerial group will buy them a meal or put them up for the night. You have no idea of all the resources I've learned over the years. I put myself or children in their situation and think, “what if it was us?”

Three guys from California needed help because their van broke down. They were musicians and had their instruments. I called places for a U-Haul after the mechanic I called said the engine had to be pulled. It was probably going to cost more than the van was worth. I sent them to NAPA for one more try at fixing it themselves.

One time a lady was driving alone to Wrangler’s campground. She was driving a big truck pulling a trailer with a horse. She had a flat tire on the inside wheel of the truck. I called everyone and everywhere I could, but could get nobody that Saturday afternoon. I finally contacted an answering service or central office for a well-known tire company. They didn’t know where Cadiz was. The minimum call was $200 for an emergency and the tire was $200. She had a tire that she could use until she could get somewhere to buy a new one, but she couldn’t lift it. She said her husband could have changed it. The rest of the group was meeting her the next day. As a last resort, she had to take the deal. She had a small white and brown dog with her.

One of the nicest men I’ve met over the years was from Goodletsville, TN. He was on his way to Wrangler’s Campground in the Land Between the Lakes. A bearing had gone out on his horse trailer and he asked if he could leave his mare behind the Tourist Center while he went back to Goodletsville to borrow a friend’s trailer. I had already left for the day by the time he got back to pick up the horse. He came back after the weekend with a bearing to fix his trailer and then take it home. He told me that when he had gone home the first time to get the friend’s trailer, he found that his friend had gone to Texas! The friend’s gate had been locked so he had to rent a trailer to come get his mare. By the time he finally made it to the campground, a day late, it was raining and his friends were getting ready to leave. He was very talkative. His wife had had trouble getting pregnant so they were very proud of their daughter and son. They now have three grandsons. He was a real gentleman.

A mother and daughter stopped in on Saturday just before closing the tourist center. They were having car problems. I called someone for her to talk to. He said it was probably the alternator. They were coming back from Georgia going to Wisconsin. It was raining so I drove them over to the Holiday Inn to spend the night. The fellow would work on the car the next day. When I came to work on Sunday at 1pm, the car was gone. I still have her name and phone number.

I have had a few people in who could not speak or hear. One couple visited several times, and we communicated by gestures or writing notes. They were a small couple; very polite and patient with me.

The Good, The Bad and The Funny

I cannot begin to name all the couples that have left their names and addresses with me and have invited us to look them up when we travel in their area. Most people are so nice and friendly. Public relations work requires you to want to know about people and want to be helpful. When it's natural for you to be interested in people and really listen, it makes your job a joy. We did get in touch with several people, had dinner and got to know their area better.

When I worked downtown many people stopped to visit, see the museum and just talk. They enjoyed seeing a hotel registration, an old fragile shopping catalog and a notebook from a grocery store with charge account information written in beautiful calligraphy. There was a short antique bed, pie safe and woodstove among other things. The log house was built in 1867 and restored in 1979 as a visitor's information center. I met the nieces of Ms. Emma Rasco the previous owner.

A lot of people are working on genealogy, and they need local information or a contact person. They also want to contact the historical society. I have been asked about any conceivable question you can think of. Remember the nude camping question?

I ask people to sign our guest register to see where they are from: only the city and state. That is a good way to start a conversation. A few refuse, afraid they might get unwanted mail. We have plenty of mail to send out to those that actually want the information. I have received so many compliments and good strokes. A few wrote notes to the Tourism Director downtown. Some have written on sign-in sheet – "thanks for friendly hostess" or "your attendant is great". They also thanked me for suggestions or help at previous visits. It's nice to be appreciated for a job you really enjoy. One couple wanted information on the Land between the Lakes National Recreation Area to take their two children. I replied verbally as well as supplying them with brochures. He refused to sign the guest register. That's OK. I never pressure them, and I thought it was a little amusing when they stopped again to use the restroom on their way home.

One unforgettable man in his 50's pulled open the door, stepped inside and flung both arms wide. He said I have lost my wife! My first thought was they were in a camper, he thought she was in it and had left her at a stop they made. He explained they were from Georgia driving 2 cars. They were taking 1 to a nephew in college in Illinois. In Clarksville they stopped at a service center to check out a noise on one of the cars, as they left they got separated. His only hope was that she could find that college in Illinois since they had no cell phones.

Over the years I have learned not to assume whether they are very young looking grandparents or older parents of young children. You also can't assume that couples are married or father and a daughter or mother and son. A couple from Burlington Iowa came into the tourist center. She was a very small lady. She was wearing tennis shoes with blue socks turned up. Her hair was gray. She looked almost Amish in appearance. She was very nice. She had on a darker gray, homemade looking, plain jumper with a little strip of crochet material at the top of her gray blouse. He looked younger with dark hair and a cap. He was very tall while she was short. I thought at first she was his mother until they started talking about going to Nashville to visit their daughter.

A couple from Clarksville shared his 59th birthday pecan pie with me. Every year a sister-in-law baked him a pecan pie and another sister-in-law bakes him a chocolate pie. They sat and ate in our covered picnic area. Since our renovation, we no longer have a shelter over our picnic tables. When I first started working here there were flowers by the tables, and there was a fenced field to gaze out over. Now, there is a service station where that field had been. It's not as pleasant a place to eat as it used to be.

We had such a good trip to the Northwest. Some of the places we visited along the way were because of suggestions from people stopping by. One of those places was Devil's Tower. I would ask about things to see in their state. They would mention places they visited on their vacation. I loved driving across South Dakota, seeing Lincoln's ear is not finished at Mt. Rushmore and the beautiful Lake at Yellowstone. We all applauded Old Faithful Geyser like it erupted just for our pleasure. The Northwest Coast is different from New England and so rugged. We saw whales and many lighthouses.

Two sisters and their mother entered the Tourist Center while their dad waited in the car. They had been in Oklahoma to their mother's sister's funeral. She had died from an aneurism. During their time there, a cousin in her mid-forties was found dead in a rental trailer at Myrtle Beach. They were going to her funeral in North Carolina. A man power washing the trailer found her dead and husband in severe shock. He was in intensive care. They did not know if he awakened and found her or had a heart attack. Their dad's sister's daughter was waiting for a liver transplant. This had been a stressful week for all of them.

A Minnesota couple going across Kentucky to Virginia to visit son in school wanted help in deciding what to see and do in Kentucky. Their compliments to me written on the sheet were thanks for being a good hostess.

There was an instant bond with a lady I met who has moved to Cadiz from California. She was reared by a great grandmother. She used china and silver, in a community that didn't care about such amenities of social behavior. After a year of college she married and had six children in 12 years, they divorced when her oldest child was 11. With no child support, she managed to put herself through college. Of course that took a lot of hard work, sacrifice and management. Ten years ago she married a man that is in the military. She plans to one day write a book on her life. Not only will it be interesting, but it will probably be a self-help book. She has no patience with young ladies who say that they cannot accomplish things because they have a child or two.

In the fall of 2007 a woman visited with me for a while, she and her husband met in Florida 25 years ago. He was from Alaska, and they have lived there all these years. She talked about how low the crime rate was in their town; they didn't lock their doors and left the keys in their cars. Now they spend part of the year in Florida and have learned that you do lock your doors.

I have mentioned about being asked about nude camping. They were a tall well-tanned couple that came into the Tourist Center. She went to the lady's room while he stopped at the desk. He said, very quietly and quickly, "Do you have nude camping in the area?" I said, "excuse me" he repeated his question a little louder, then I answered, "we have a lot of nice campgrounds but you have to keep your clothes on". My thought was, "I bet they have no tan lines!"

A couple, who now live in Ohio, told me an interesting story. They had grown up in Tennessee, going to the same school and church together. The woman's mother had sent her to Nashville to go to High School, and the couple had lost touch with each other. They eventually both married other people and had children. Her marriage had only lasted 5 years, and she had never remarried. She had been an only child and said that her father had prayed for someone to help take care of her after her parents died. The man was in the military and had been married for 35 years. Then his wife decided that she wanted a different lifestyle. After they divorced, he looked up his current wife. They have been married for over six years. Her dad has passed away, and her mom lives with them. His parents have been deceased for a long time, but he has a sister in Tennessee. She was in a car accident when she was seventeen and is living in a nursing home.

A very interesting lady I met was writing a book and researching different areas she had lived as a child. She stayed a long time and talked a lot of the closeness she had with her brother. Her brother was very sick and – the mother was pregnant with her at the time, while the mother sat by the bedside, the brother drew strength from her in the womb. She knew when her brother was hurt overseas during a war – and he knew when she was ill in a hospital. They each sensed this distinctly without being told. Her mother died from a brain tumor. She always said if she could come back in another life, she would like to be a poodle and live with her daughter. Years later this lady was given a poodle and it, too, died of a brain tumor. She said it was the best little dog she ever had. She took care of her brother when he was sick and died. He suggested she write a book on their unusual family.

Another lady was visiting her family east of Bowling Green. She was very distraught as she paced in front of the desk. She had come from Georgia for a class reunion and was on her way home. She said “my husband shot my son”. My daughter called and said he would survive. The lady said nothing should make you try to kill your son no matter what they do. The son was an alcoholic and probably pushed her husband to the limit.

One day Mr. Wilson did not feel up to working. I had worked for him before or we would trade days, but this was one to remember. We only had 1 extra roll of toilet tissue; I had ordered some that would come in soon. Still you get a little apprehensive. One of the commodes would not flush; the chain was off in the chain tank. I had fixed it before. I always check the bathrooms for cleanliness. Within a short period of time, someone had left a cigarette burning on the floor behind the commode. I had to fix the chain on the commode. When I went to check the men's room, someone had thrown our only spare roll of toilet tissue in the men's commode. It was soggy and beyond use. I got it out with a commode brush and threw it in the trash. Then someone locked the lady's room and closed the bathroom door as they came out. I had to use a nail to push in the center hole to unlock the door. What a day – I was not even supposed to work that day.

We have also had interesting times with our mice, mostly in the fall. One day a sick one kept coming into the main room leaning or staggering & gagging (kidding)! It would fall down, I would think it was dead and it would get up again.

A humorous story from a lady several years ago... The couple was in their 60's and they were talking about their trip on Amtrak. She said the bathroom was so tiny, and she is quite heavy, so she had to back in through the door. While sitting on the commode instead of reaching back and flushing the commode she turned on the shower. She had yelled for her husband to help.

A folk singer from Wisconsin told a funny story about his mother and her new husband. His mother had left her purse at church again, not the first time this had happened. The preacher called and told him it was in his office. She sent her husband to pick it up. People for the second service were coming in as he was going out the door. A couple of the guys kidded him about carrying a purse. It embarrassed him, so he stuck it inside his coat.

A policeman across the street saw him, several questions and explanations later he was able to go home and take his wife her purse. The family enjoys telling this story.

A very nice couple from Virginia was in the Tourist Center. I've always compared the shape of Virginia to that of Kentucky. Our lakes are in the western area of the state and the mountains, in the eastern. They had never been to Kentucky before and needed a lot of information. I have lived in the area of Virginia near Washington D.C., but have traveled all over the state. They were well informed and planned on seeing a lot of Kentucky before they returned home.

I had a nice conversation with a man who was stationed at Fort Campbell. He had been in the military and had been overseas a couple of times. He was now a civilian contractor and still went overseas on occasion. He was so interesting to talk to that, after I closed the Tourist Center for the evening, we stood on the porch and talked for a while longer. He was a Cherokee whose mother had been a Caucasian. His dad was full Cherokee and this presented him with a problem of language, when he was a child. When he was at school, he had been expected to speak English. He would get spanked if he didn't. But if he spoke English at home, he would get spanked by his Grandmother for not speaking Cherokee. He said the spankings were more akin to beatings. He decided later that he would marry a Caucasian so that his children could fit in with both worlds. He said that, in the long run, that approach had worked out well for his siblings and himself. He was certainly a polite, well mannered, person.

A very enthusiastic new father came in one day. They were originally from Nashville and had recently moved to Clarksville. He wanted to know all about the area and showed me the baby pictures, they were triplets. The two identical boys had light hair, blue eyes and very fair complexions. The girl had dark hair and eyes; they were conceived via in vitro fertilization. He was a nice guy, a salesman and his wife was a school counselor. She had bed rest for the last 5 months of her pregnancy and now she was a stay at home Mom. He said she would probably go back to work eventually, he thought she would probably like to now.

Several years ago I had quite a conversation with a very talkative, kind of weird type of man. I mostly just listened, he left his name and phone number; thought my son might get in touch with him for a job as my son was relocating from California to Kentucky. I don't think so... He said he was a millionaire or close to it. He said he was 44 years old and had been self-sufficient since the age of 6. He had a leg off below the knee. He called his dad something I won't repeat. His parents were divorced. His Mom was in her early 70's and he has an older sister. She made good grades in school but he didn't, yet he is the "smart" one. He was beginning to look for a wife, no time to wine and dine, just going to ask someone to marry him. He had odd ideas. He sleeps in snatches, 3-4 hours, just taking naps.

I had an interesting conversation in January of 2008, a 56 year old man from North Carolina knew someone I had known from Golden Pond; he had served in Vietnam with him. He sent his son to law school and had been on 3 cruises. We discussed my two cruises from Naples, Italy to New York and to Alaska. His wife of 36 years was serving time in jail for forgery. She had worked in a museum. His wife said she was innocent, but he thinks she is guilty. This fellow has several convenience stores and also works with a mission to give homeless boys jobs. Ten of these boys grew up to become preachers and another ten had been killed.

A lady originally from Illinois but had been living in Alabama shared a story. Her husband has recently been transferred to Indiana. Her mother had died a few months ago, so they needed to be closer to her dad in Southern Illinois. A friend had bought a purse in Savannah. She didn't remember the name of the store, but knew it was in the vicinity of Paula Dean's Restaurant. It had a picture of dachshund on it; she's into saving dogs, especially that one. She wanted a purse like that. She called Paula Dean's Restaurant and described the store and purse, relaying what the woman had told her. The lady that answered the phone said she knew exactly the store she wanted. She gave her the name and even looked up the phone number for her. She then asked the woman if she were Paula Dean because she sounded like her and the woman answered, "Why, honey, it sure is".

I enjoyed a very smart little boy in May of 2007; he was with his Grandpa. I'm assuming he was adopted because he was oriental or maybe one parent was. He was in the moving van with his grandpa, while his parents were in another vehicle going to Fort Campbell. He spoke very well for his age. Asked several questions about things we had in our display cases.

On the opposite end I had a little girl who practically bounced off of the walls. The mother was pregnant and the girl about 7 years old. The mom didn't agree with her teachers that she needed medication, so she was going to home school her. I can't imagine how that would work out. She was into everything and running around like crazy. She would not pay any attention to her mother. She even jumped onto my lap while I was sitting behind my desk! She was really wild.

A 52 year old woman from Monroe, Washington, 35 miles east of Seattle has been married for 23 years. She helped her husband through school but couldn't live with her husband anymore. Over the years he had been a little overbearing. He had wanted everything his way and was quite a selfish person. She had always worked, kept her mouth shut and put up with it. After menopause she had no more blockers to keep her mouth shut; she just says what she has been keeping inside all these years. She had a big house with lots of land (5 acres) and was going through a divorce. Both of them still lived in the same house, her upstairs and him down. A real estate agent wanted $16,000 to sell the house, so she is planning on getting her own license to sell it herself. The stories that people tell me allow me to see their points of view. Sometimes, I wonder what things they couldn't share. We all keep things hidden.

In October 2008 a woman from Illinois was going to Alabama. She walked a little unsteady, hopefully, she wasn't drinking. Her husband was retired military. They were in Europe for 9 years; their 2 daughters grew up there. She was young looking (or she looked young in appearance), but tired and a little confused (disoriented). She was upset because her 3 year old grandson had suffered 3rd degree burns. He had been left to do his bath by himself. The water was way too hot when he stepped in, he slipped and he fell. She was anxious about him and angry about his being left alone to take a bath. She was going to care for her other grandchildren while her daughter stayed at the hospital to take care of the little boy.

I met a woman from Illinois who was on crutches. Her doctor had done surgery on a cyst or something and put the cast on too tight. She told him it was tight but he said that it was "fine" and increased her medication. He then left town for a few days. A nurse looked at it when she complained then got a second doctor who agreed the cast had to come off. Her main nerve had been killed. After several years there was some feeling in her toes. Two years before, a child had experienced similar problems on her arm (she found this out afterward), the arm had swollen and turned dark and the ER called this same doctor. He said that it was just an overprotective mother yet the child has a crippled arm today.

In the 1960s a woman and her 6 year old daughter went to Alaska for a month and a half, they ended up staying 8 years. Some people in a camper wanted someone to travel with them and share expenses. She checked them out and felt safe enough to travel with them. This woman said that her daughter had trained her horse to do better than Roy Rogers horse "Trigger". A carnival group from Florida saw her in Alaska and invited her to join them. As she was only 14 the mother traveled with her to Florida. She is originally from South Dakota but spends the winter in Florida; the daughter is now about 40 years old. I don't know whether or not she is still with the carnival.

One early summer day a cute, energetic young woman came into the tourist center. While her husband waited in the car, she told me that they were from South Dakota and were on their way to Florida. As they had traveled over the lakes on I-24 she told her husband that she would like to stay on the lake instead of going to Nashville, TN, where they had reservations. I recommended Lake Barkley State Park. Her face fell and she said, "Oh, we want something nice." I told her it was a very nice resort and described it for her. I then placed a call for her and she made a reservation. The next morning, she bounded up the steps to tell me that it was very nice and they had made a reservation for later in the year to come back for a week.

Three couples came in that were going to a Vietnam Veterans reunion in Minnesota. The three women were very talkative. Two of the couples were from Florida and one was from North Carolina. One man was a HOOT! He said an amusing quote.... He said "I went to night school so I can't see in the day time."

In June 2010 a very friendly couple stopped by. They were from Aurora, Illinois. He was originally from Elgin, Illinois where my uncle Bob lived for years and taught English and Journalism in a High school near there. I had enjoyed visiting Bob and eating in a French restaurant in Chicago. This fellow was a semi-retired lawyer, and they spent their winters in Florida. They discussed how people would run over you in the grocery stores with their carts. I was reading The Shack by Wm. Paul Young at the time. She had also read it and we discussed the book. He left his business card with me in the event that I ever needed a lawyer.

One interesting conversation was with a woman from Laurel, Delaware. She was going to Albany, Kentucky to visit a pen pal. She read in a magazine over 15 years ago where a 15 year old girl wanted a recipe for goat cheese. She sent the recipe and that started the writing back and forth. She said the girl was a hillbilly, had these goats and didn't know what to do with all that milk, back then. This is why she was writing for the recipe to begin with. The 15 year old had a baby in the following year and her mother raised the grandchild who is now a teenager. The woman that came in here was now 65 to 68 years of age, and the pen pal is in her early thirties; she's been married and divorced twice but no more children. She went to college on the ROTC program and has been to Iraq and Germany, and is now home on leave. She was so excited that they were going to meet for the first time in the more than 15 years that they had been corresponding.

In January 2008 a very nice couple from southern Illinois wanted to talk. We had a great conversation and they stayed from 8:45am to 9:25am. We talked about their trip to Alaska and Hawaii, comparing it to my cruise to Alaska and living in Hawaii almost three years. They haven't been to the northeast yet. I had lived in Massachusetts and talked about our trip the fall of 2006, to visit all the northeast states, including Maine the only state that I hadn't visited at that time. We talked about who might win the Presidential nomination. They raised New Zealand or was it Australian white rabbits for show?

In the spring of 2008 a man shared part of his life with me. His grandparents on both sides were from Germany. He was the youngest of 5 boys. His mother died at his birth and his aunt reared him until he was 15, then he went to an orphanage in Minnesota. There were 500 children separated by sex and age. He said that orphanage has been closed for years. He said he had a wonderful home with his aunt. He now lives in Indiana but loves gong to Renfro valley in Kentucky. While he lived at the orphanage, the matron of his cottage would bring in her radio at night and they would listen to the gospel music from Renfro valley. He talked on about what happened to his other brothers and how he was the caretaker to the oldest brother until his death in this year.

I do meet all kinds of people. This has been a very interesting job. In the fall of 2009 a couple from San Diego came in; they were likeable people. He soon went back to the car. She really needed to dish; get it out. He was really big with a huge stomach. She was not real heavy just chubby, blondish grey; a very nice looking older woman. She was really on a rampage. He had worked 33 years as an engineer and done a lot of traveling while she stayed at home with their 3 children. They hadn't been able to do things with couples as he was always gone. The kids were always happy to see him when he did get home. She was always the disciplinarian. He had been retired 2 years and these were supposed to be the "golden years". He's a Pisces. Just drive to the destination and get home; not much stopping along the way to see things. She had really looked forward to traveling, but on this trip she has missed so much that she really wanted to see. She really wanted to see the quilt museum in Paducah and get her uncle a Kentucky souvenir. Like bourbon from a distillery or anything "Kentucky". Now they were leaving Kentucky, she was taking pictures from the car window. She just really needed to get it all out .... She was really on a rampage. I could relate, I too have gone on a trip with a Pisces, took pictures out of the windows and we also didn't stop very often.

One day in March of 2008 a nice couple from New Hampshire came in. They had been in Paducah to visit the quilt museum. She enjoyed this since she herself is a quilter. They also saw the river front area including the flood wall murals. They were on their way back to Bowling Green where they were staying. They had ordered their new red Corvette convertible from the factory in Bowling Green. I had told her she better watch him when they go home to New Hampshire as he was an attractive man in his 60's. She said she'd put a homing device on it. He said they would have to wait until April to drive it because the snow was so deep in New Hampshire, when they had left there the snow was up to the signs. It appeared that the signs were sitting on the snow with no posts showing, at all. They got a personal tour of the Corvette Factory and a free entrance to the museum for allowing their car to be put in the museum for 2-4 weeks; I've forgotten exactly which. They got it cheaper than from a dealer but nothing off for displaying it in the Museum, except the tour and museum entrance. They were driving their new Corvette and I went out to see it. (It was very pretty...)

A very talkative fellow came in from Leeton, Missouri, population 700. He said it was close to Kansas City, Missouri. He was stopping by the museum in Hopkinsville. He was checking out Dr. Venable's family, of whom he was related. He had Lyon's disease, which was really affecting his health. He looked healthy though; about 45 – 55ish. He used to be a band director. He now owns the local newspaper. He talked about their museum of the 20's and 30's. A local blacksmith had gone to Paris and taken wonderful pictures. They have hundreds of them on display in the museum. He was so enthusiastic it made you want to visit their museum.

A fellow living in Murray stopped in several times on his way to Fort Campbell. He was 82, but looked younger. No wrinkles and dark hair which he said he didn't dye. His first wife left him after 20 years to "...find herself...". He had been in the Army for 4 years and the

Air Force for 16 years. He liked the Air Force better. He said the Air Force had better food, less working hours, etc. They had 4 or 5 children together. His second wife was almost 19 years old while he was 50. When she went to college, she left him on the advice of a friend. He was very short and walked slow, but he claimed to be healthy, said his doctor wished he himself had such good blood work results, etc. His third wife was a socialite. Her Mom had made her promise to take care of her in her old age. After being married to him for 5 years, her Mom insisted that she divorce him. She did so in order to get all of her mothers' money. She stayed with him another 5 years, because they loved each other. She continued to call him several times a day even after she moved out. He was married to his last wife for 16 years. She left him because she wanted to spend her time with her son and grandchildren. He liked to travel. He has been in 50 countries and all of the States. His fourth wife asked him, "When you married your first wife, why didn't you give me a chance?". He said, "I didn't think I had a chance with you." She was a Sherriff's daughter and 3 years younger. She said, "You always had a chance... ". Now that he was alone again, he was looking for another wife. He had known his last one when they were young. He said he didn't want a fat wife because they looked uncomfortable. The next time I saw him, he had just gotten out of the hospital in N.C. He had been making a trip to the N.E. and had gotten as far as his daughter's, sold his home in Murray ... and didn't know what he was going to do. He stopped by again in 2011, he was driven by his son, and he was currently living near a sister in Paducah. He was now 86 years old.

I can't begin to write about all the people riding motorcycles. Guys on Harley Davidsons think there is no other like it. A guy loves his BMW- others think their Goldwing's are the best. Some couples ride together – some women want their own. They ride to Arizona, California, and Canada. They love to go to rallies. Sometimes there are several riding along together. I have had a little experience riding myself; I prefer the two lane roads to the interstate. It is fun, but I feel very venerable out there when there is a lot of traffic. Usually there is not so much fast traffic and big trucks on the two lane roads.

I try to steer away from much conversation about politics or especially religion, except when people are staying in the area I do invite them to our church. I had several conversations about how America is changing and how other countries are "buying out" America.

A lot of people from Wisconsin and Minnesota stop in. They have beautiful pastures, fields and barns. I talk about our trip to the Wisconsin Dells and touring the House on the Rock. I have never seen such a collection of everything as they have in there.

The lakes are beautiful in Minnesota, and I enjoyed the mall of America. I discussed touring St. Paul's Cathedral with people from that area.

A fellow came in who was born and grew up in Sault Saint Marie; we discussed the upper peninsula of Michigan and what a great trip our friends planned with us. We had lunch at the hotel on Mackinac Island. The pictured rocks boat tour was wonderful and driving all around the upper peninsula of Michigan was a great experience. En route we stayed in Frankenmuth, a wonderful town north of Flint, Michigan. It looks like a Swiss village. I love to travel and working here gives me an opportunity to help people. It gives me a chance to compare places we've been and find new places to go. I've always promoted Western Kentucky and this job gives me the opportunity to tell people about it.

I've discussed the Florida Keys with guests several times. I tell people how much we enjoyed our drive down the Keys, but I was always surprised at the lack of nice beaches there. When you drive to Naples or Ft. Myers, FL, you'll find a lot of nice beaches.

People from upstate New York don't have anything good to say about New York City. I've always wanted to go and when we got the opportunity to go with the bank group (the bank organized the trip and rented a tour bus) we really had a good time. Some of the things we did were seeing a Broadway show, ground zero, had a step on guide to tour the city, and enjoyed taking pictures of the Wall Street District.

One sad situation, two older ladies were sisters-in–law and widowed. The lady from Iowa had married the Florida lady's brother. The Iowa lady had been to the Keys to visit her son. She picked up the Florida lady on the way back to Iowa. She got confused about how to get to I-57. She said this would be her last trip. She was getting too old. The Florida lady said she really appreciated her because she wasn't able to drive. She was going to visit grandchildren in Iowa. Her baby girl died and her son died at age 50. She had a son in Florida. They both talked a lot about family. Her sister-in-law was her only resource to be able to visit the grandchildren in Iowa.

Then there was Polly S. from Illinois, who came in newly divorced. She was recovering from an aneurism and didn't realize how long it would take to drive to Saratoga, FL. She was not in very good shape. Her husband and step son were both mistreating her. She didn't get the papers to appear in court, because her mother had put them away in a drawer and she was in Florida at a women's shelter. She had thought that she and her husband were trying to decide on working out their problems. So he got everything. They had owned a $175,000 home and the husband was elated over that. He did take her in after her surgery since her parents weren't well. The person she spoke with on the phone sounded like more than a mere friendship. She said that she had been in a women's shelter there. Her hair was beginning to grow back on the sides of her head where it had been shaven or cut.

One couple really liked to talk about their travels. They were from Minneapolis, MN. They drove through the Land between the Lakes area. They had been hunting in North Dakota and had been to Montana and Wyoming. Their next trip would be to Washington and Oregon. I've enjoyed my trips there as well. It has the rugged coastline and a lot of lighthouses. We saw a whale putting on a show.

Another couple the same day had lived in Alaska for 30 years. They raised 5 children there; they said it really grows on you. They just loved it. He worked with caterpillars. They lived 5 years in Juneau, but mostly outside of Anchorage and Fairbanks. He says it gets 50 below zero and spit freezes before it hits the ground in Anchorage. They said there was too much rain in Juneau. I shared about the cruise we took, we stopped in Juneau, and it did rain that day. But the weather was nice in Ketchikan and Skagway. We went into Glacier Bay and it was just beautiful. This was in September. I would not want to live there but would enjoy a trip across to see more of Alaska, especially Denali National Park.

In the spring of 2008 I received a nice compliment from a young looking 82 year old. He was a World War II veteran. He and his wife were from Missouri. His brother and wife were from Michigan. His brother was 72. Their sister age 86 was small and frail. They were on their way to Lake Lure in North Carolina to meet another brother from Florida. I have been passed there many times going to Gastonia, North Carolina. The lady from Michigan really held on and took good care of her husband's sister. The fellow from Missouri said, "I was a natural for this job, so cordial". He had made the trip to DC for the World War II veterans. It's nice to have compliments when you try to do your job well. Public relations work requires you to want to know about people, be helpful and interested in them. There is a difference between interested and nosey. I have received many compliments both orally and written.

A guy from Illinois was in talking about humming birds. He said his neighbors built a big house in the middle of a field with lots of acreage and no trees. She fixed 70 lbs. of sugar in 2007 for those hummingbirds. He said she is not one to exaggerate. I remembered when he was talking how much my mother enjoyed watching them on her porch in her later years. This brought back memories of how I too used to fix sugar water to put in the feeders.

One day a fellow on a motorcycle came in. A lot of motorcycle riders stop by; couples, groups and some by themselves. This particular man works in Florida on cars with a friend in winter, and works in construction building houses in Indiana in summer. He was a young 59, maybe that was because he kept so busy.

A man originally from Chicago, moved to Kuttawa several years ago. He talked about how fast people drove through the residential area. They drive fast on my road as well. He said they hit the squirrels and turtles, paying no attention. He was very riled up. His daughter is a graphic artist that works for a place that makes signs. They had pictures of different animals put on the signs. He put the signs in different yards, out on the hills, close to the roads where they could be seen. He said he is trying to get people to "get the message". He said, "I'm a native now and I want to protect the wild life". He left one of the signs with me.

One day a woman with her 3 children came in. A teenage daughter and two boys ages 10 and 12. She was originally from California and her husband from Eastern Kentucky. They had lived in Hopkinsville for 4 years, but hadn't been anywhere around the lakes. They didn't know anything about this area. She wanted information to take some visitors places. It was difficult to believe, but they had just been busy with the kids, involved with them. She was well informed by the time she left.

One day 3 women came in from outside of Nashville Tn. The 2 older women were sisters and the one in her 40's was one of the lady's daughters. We had a nice, long conversation. The youngest one said that after 911 she and her husband lost their jobs with Motorola, in Arizona. Now, they live 6 months in New Zealand, in a motor home. And visit with family and friends for 6 months in the United States. She said the 6 months pass fast when you have his and her families to visit. They will probably buy a motor home to live in for the United States too. She loves New Zealand especially after living in the hot desert of Arizona. She hadn't had a desire to visit Australia but probably will eventually. They've enjoyed seeing Ireland and England. Australia, England and Ireland would be favorite places for me to go. In June of 2008, a nice couple from Sacramento, CA stopped by. They moved there many years ago from Minneapolis, Minnesota. They love the weather. They were on their way to visit their daughter and family in Knoxville, Tennessee.

Several years ago, a man was walking, trying to get rides, from the eastern part of the U.S. to a state out west. He was of average size and was very enthusiastic about being here. All he had was what he was wearing: two shirts, two pairs of pants, etc. You could see the hem of the pants below the top pair. He asked me for nothing. Usually they want work, money, a meal or a place to stay. He was so happy to be here that he kissed the wall and laid a dead butterfly on my desk. He walked around, very excitedly. I really wasn't comfortable being alone with him. If he had stayed longer he may have asked for help. As I prayed for a law enforcement person to appear, a patrolman actually did drive up. The patrolman was having trouble with his phone and had stopped to use mine. As he entered, the excited man went into the restroom. I explained the situation to the officer and asked if he would hang out for a bit. After using my phone the officer went outside and waited in his patrol car. When the man came out of the restroom he saw that the patrolman was still there and he left immediately. I got the feeling that, for whatever reason, he wanted to avoid the law.

I met an attractive young lady from Seattle, Washington. She works for a company that sells boat lifts, to keep your boat out of the water while at the boat dock. I gave her a lot of information on this area. She said she had sold to people in Alabama and Tennessee but not Kentucky. We discussed my trip to Seattle and eating at the Space Needle.

A nice young fellow from Connecticut was roller blading from Yorktown Virginia to San Francisco, California. He had been going to college in New Hampshire. He was so nice and polite, he had a big backpack. Surprisingly I have met so many different people over the years, traveling across country usually on bicycle or even hitchhiking, instead of the comfort of a car. This was the first I had met on in line skates.

A lot of times 2 or 3 groups will join in on conversations. One talkative lady from Davenport, Iowa practically told us her life story. Her conversation ranged from her marrying into a Greek family and her area not accepting immigrants well, to her not being able to find a Baskin Robins when she was traveling. Her two daughters were dark like her husband, and short like her with her Irish chin. She was blond, natural or not. The guy taking part in the conversation was from Georgia. He had bought 90 acres in Clarksville. He would eventually put in a hunting lodge. He was a hunter, real country, a Man's man.

A very different type of guy from Georgia worked for the state and genealogy. He is now retired, but writes a column on genealogy for a newspaper. His information was quite different from other people that have been in researching or trying to find relatives in the area and local information. He checked out one side of his family with DNA; a swab in the mouth is sent to a place that keeps it on record and you pay $200. It can be checked against other people interested in tracking down their families. You may be matched or not with people of the same name in other states. You may also find relatives of different names that match your DNA. It can get costly to pay $200 each time; more extensive testing costs more than $200. He has done research for a former president and his wife.

One day a nice couple from Fort Worth, Texas came in. They had been to Metropolis, Illinois where they were both originally from. They were celebrating their 50th wedding anniversary with their families. They are glad that all 3 children and all the grandchildren live close to them in Texas. She talked a lot of personal stuff about her family, especially a brother that is now 80 and a disappointment. He did not have the values the rest of the family had. She talked more after her husband went to the car.

I witnessed a strange thing one day. A woman was in wanting information about cashing a company check. She said she had two kids needing to eat before she could get to Paducah to Wal-Mart, to cash the check. After solving her problem, a local business would cash it, she started out the driveway in front of the service station. All of a sudden the trunk opened and an older teenage girl climbed out and got in the car. Was she playing a trick on her Mom? "You don't know where I am!" Did the one in the car tell her mother the girl was hiding in the trunk and the mother was going to let her think she was going to leave with her in there? Or would she let the girl think she would leave her behind not knowing where she was? It was very strange to watch through the window.

One couple from Glasgow, KY, had lots of stories. It was the second marriage for both. She had married at age 14. He has children and grandchildren. He drove Amish people around to different states. That was another insight into another way of life.

There have been a lot of discussions over the years about various surgeries and injuries that people have had. One sad story a lady told was about a friend who was very active and liked to go places, but she had very bad bones. She had to have knee surgery and it went great. The surgery on the second knee did not go well. After 10 surgeries there was no bone left, she had to have the leg amputated above the knee. She said the family had made an invalid out of her. They keep her home and do everything for her. Her daughter and family have put a mobile home in next to the parent's house.

One couple that came in had been out to Utah, they were on their way to their home in North Carolina. She had been to all the States too, so we had a lot to talk about, comparing where we had been. Her first husband had died. Her second husband didn't think he would like to take bus tours. I've enjoyed the three I've taken to New York, New Orleans and New England. She really enjoyed bus tours and thought if he were to try one he would like them too. They had been 14 days on the road. She had a bus tour planned with her daughter and granddaughter to New York.

A man from Tennessee stopped by with a dog named "Baby". He was in love with a woman for 40 years. With the complications of life they both went through two marriages before they could be together. She was his fiancee for four years. Don't ask! She was taking care of her mother and her dog. The fiancé had oral surgery and died soon afterwards. He thinks an infection of some kind; they told him complications from pneumonia. He inherited the dog, he always wanted to bring her to the Land between Lakes but they never got to make the trip.

In the spring of 2008 a woman was riding a bicycle from Olympia, Washington to Illinois to visit friends. She said she felt relatively safe. Another woman here that day said most crimes are done by people who know the women they kill. (Certainly, not always?). This was the second woman to stop in who was riding a bicycle from the State of Washington. The first one was college age. She said her family was worried about her riding that far. She was going to New England, this was several years ago. Sometimes she camped out, other times she stayed in motels. She picked places where she felt safe to camp out.

A coach bus driver from Missouri has stopped in several times; this fellow said he enjoys his job. He spends several days a year in Branson. He stays free and the food and shows are free as long you're in uniform. He said he could write a book about each trip.

I met an interesting lady from Newburgh, IN. She was a retired school teacher whose husband had left her and their three children. There was an 8 or 9 year old boy, and two girls, one of whom was 15 and the other was high school age. He left for work one day with a cup of coffee in his hand and never returned. One of the daughters found him years later living in Nevada. Apparently his cabinet business had been in trouble and he just walked away. She'd been married to a second husband for 21 years. She speaks in terms of 1st life and 2nd life when speaking of friends or happenings in her life.

Another guy from N.C. said he and his wife are now retired. They lived in Utah at one time. He has his masters and doctorate. He wrote a lot of things for work and thought about writing a book of short stories. But he's like me, can write the facts, but is not good at spicing up the facts or extending beyond what actually happened.

A fellow has stopped in several times in the fall, as he drives a car from Nebraska to Florida for two women; they were two sisters who had inherited a "condo" from their dad. In May he flies down and drives the car back to Nebraska. He says he gets $500.00. I'm not sure if he means each way or round trip. The women always fly. He's 72, a very likable, friendly man. He either retired from the airlines or his son works for them. Either way he flies cheap. He likes to compare how farmers in Kentucky farm to how it's done in Nebraska.

I had a long interesting conversation with a guy in his mid-50's. We covered many subjects. He'd been married 25 years, with two sons. His wife wanted a divorce. He had built them a nice house in a subdivision, which she wanted, instead of a log cabin in the woods so he could hunt. He talked about his older brother who was in the National Guard, which was supposed to guard the United States, being called to Vietnam. His close buddies were killed at Hamburger Hill the week after the brother was called home to attend their grandfather's funeral. This fellow has been the caregiver for his mother when she needed him. She had died the previous year in her 80's. He has land in this area and is intending to build on it.

I do hear all kinds of stories. Some leave you thinking about them or someone they talked about. This woman from Minnesota was going to a family reunion in Alabama. She divorced her husband after their two boys were grown. She met her second husband through a church group for divorced people. That marriage lasted only two years. That's when she moved to Minnesota. He left her with a lot of bills to pay. She met her third husband through an internet type program; they filled out paper that eliminated a lot of questions. She is a State Executive agent retired from Alabama. Now she lacks only

4 years and can retire from Minnesota. Her family all live in Alabama and she has one grandchild. Her husband is willing to move somewhere between Minnesota and Alabama. She teaches a home economic type course to handicapped, deaf and foreign people. She has interpreters. She was quite an interesting lady to talk with. She left Minnesota the day the bridge in Minneapolis collapsed. She was very concerned about her neighbor. When she talked with her husband last night, the neighbor's car wasn't home; the woman drove over that bridge every day. She was going to call and check on her...so of course I still wonder about the neighbor.

It's amazing how fast accidents or events happen that change your life. A couple from Florida came in that were in their late 40s or early 50s. They were building a log home. He was only a few feet off the ground when the ladder slipped and somehow cut off part of his foot. The doctors didn't want to try to save the part that was cut off even though he wanted them to try to save all of his foot. They took grafts from a hip and inserted a vein. At first part of the foot died. A year or two later, they're still trying to save that foot. A boot helps him walk.

In September 2010 two guys came in with bicycles on top of their vehicle. Friends in Mississippi had told them how nice the Land between the Lakes was, and to ride the canal loop. I told them the history of the Land between the Lakes National Recreation Area which they found quite interesting. One is doing the triathlon in September 2011 in Beijing. The following day three women came in with two bicycles on their vehicle. They were headed to Tennessee. Two were going to ride about 150 miles or so, on the Natchez Trace. One would be following in the

The entrance to the Land between the Lakes National Recreation Area.

vehicle. The trail or trace starts a little south of Nashville, through Alabama to Natchez.

I enjoyed reminiscing with a very nice couple who had stopped in to call and verify their reservation at a hotel in the Nashville area. They lived in Pierre, South Dakota, just north of where Bill and I drove after leaving the Welcome Center on the Missouri River, in the Louis & Clark area. Originally from Connecticut, they had lived in Kentucky at one time. Now retired, they had moved back to Connecticut, for a while, and then moved back to South Dakota. They were on their way to visit their daughter and grandchildren in South Carolina.

An unmarried couple from Nashville came in. They just take day trips together. He is originally from Norfolk Virginia and is a song writer. She is originally from New Orleans but now living in Nashville. She didn't know about John James Audubon's connection to Kentucky until moving to Tennessee and visiting the John James Audubon State Park in Henderson KY. She only knew about his connection to New Orleans, he lived there part of the year. Her goal was to visit all the state parks in Kentucky.

A couple came in one beautiful day asking about the antique stores. They were very talkative, especially the woman. She mentioned that her first husband had died when she was in her 40's. She thought the best part of her life was over. She started making stuffed teddy bears as a hobby. She gave them to friends, later joined a crafts group, and started displaying and selling them. She is now 79 and married to a man a few years younger, her life has really turned around. What started as a hobby has become a business. She's been to New York in craft shows with people from all over the world. She left me with several words of wisdom. Among them, life does go on and can be very good.

A fellow from Texas came in for information in an RV. He had a business about 20 years, working 80 to 90 hours per week. So instead of 40 years at 40 hours, he worked hard for 20 years. His business was office equipment, especially long shelves for doctor's offices and libraries. Now he and his wife travel all over. He was interested in learning about Kentucky, especially our area since he had not been to Kentucky before.

On one of my days off, a co-worker was covering the Tourist Center. A very upset man came in needing to call someone to help him. He said he had left his dog in the car after it had broken down. He got so angry after calling several people and not getting the response he wanted that he completely tore up the old rotary dial phone that we had. He had a knife with him, and he then locked himself in the storage room. The attendant on duty called the police. It took two police officers to get him out of the storage room. They arrested him and later he was transferred to the mental hospital about 20 miles from here. The attendant on duty called me at home since I was to be working the next day. We heard that the man had escaped from the hospital, and we were afraid that he might come back after the address book he'd left behind. I said, "Oh, great! You make him angry, then he'll come after me!" He also might come back to retrieve his dog, if that story was true. I felt a lot better when I heard that they had caught him a short time later, headed east.

A man visited in July 2007 that was really full of himself. How much to believe, I don't know. He sat for about an hour talking in between my other visitors. He claimed to be in military security. He had on spit shine boots, shorts and a tee shirt. He had a beard and appeared clean. He had a shiny scar that looked burned, where he said a tattoo had been removed from his arm. He supposedly spoke several languages. He liked Lichtenburg, where he said is between Austria and Germany, but a city in itself like the Vatican. He hasn't married but has a daughter by an American woman, says she's not his and a son by a German woman. He paid child support. His family lives in the Louisville area and owned a company that his daughter invested in and maybe she made other investments as well. Anyway he said she made millions then lost it. Her mother shot his car up a few years ago, blaming him for the daughter losing the money. He said "how was I to blame?" The daughter is pregnant and his mother's family is giving her a shower. He said he has nothing to do with his family and has seen the daughter only 2 or 3 times. He told me he has had other tattoos removed from his hand and arm with a salt solution which leaves no scar; and this one will also look good. He says it will tan and blend in. I thought all tattoo removal left scars. He predicted that Barak Obama will be our President and will cut social security. He said he's going to Afghanistan; he can fly any kind of plane and has never had a license. There was more but this is enough. He should write a book and maybe title it "Active Imagination".

A family who lived in Whitehorse, Alaska stopped by the Tourist Center. The couple had been to Georgia for a few days while his parents in Evansville kept the children. She said they absolutely loved it in the Yukon. I can't imagine anyone living there by choice. I asked if he was in the military. She said no, but didn't say what kind of work he did. Only the wife came inside. She said that there were a lot of things to do there year round. She said there has to be to keep people there, but again, said that they loved living there. I mentioned our cruise to Alaska and she asked if we had stopped in Skagway. We had, and I told her how cute our tour guide had been. The guide had said that in the winter people painted the inside of their houses, read, or did other indoor things. My guest agreed and said that Whitehorse was just a little north of Skagway. I later looked it up on the map and sure enough, it was just a little north of where we had been. It wasn't too cold when we were there in September.

Several families with the last name of Trigg have stopped in over the years. Of course they find being in a county named Trigg fascinating. One family was on their way to a large Trigg family reunion. There are always shirts sold each October for our annual Ham Festival. These guys went into Cadiz to buy all the Trigg County Ham Festival shirts they could find.

Wanda in front of Ham Festival display at the Information Center.

A woman and her husband were staying at the bed and breakfast on Main St. She was very excited to get any information about Trigg County. She was doing genealogy research on her maiden name of Trigg. Her father was related to Colonel Stephen Trigg, for whom this county was named. Her father had been well known in Boston. Quite a bit was published about him when he passed away. She had just attended her 50th class reunion and several people mentioned reading about him.

Several days later, a woman, whose family was staying at Barkley Lodge, came in. Her husbands' grandparents were Triggs from England. She had never met a Trigg in person. She was a writer and had published several books. She wrote down the name, city and state of the Triggs that had been in a week earlier and was going to try and contact them via the internet. She said that the Triggs from England were related to a duke or some nobleman. Maybe there was a connection.

A young couple was hitch hiking in front of the tourist center. In my opinion they were ridiculously dressed to be expecting someone to give them a ride. Apparently people had. They had gone from Missouri to Michigan, down to Eastern Kentucky and were now on their way back to a farm in Missouri. He wrote down a name of a town I couldn't find listed in the Atlas. She didn't come in but sat on the porch step. They both had back packs. He was a good looking guy with dreadlocks and nice blue eyes. He had on a tee shirt, his pants cut off at the knees (with lots of ravels), a lot of patches and one big hole in the seat. She had her hair piled way up on top, a skimpy little brown top with most of her back bare, a long skirt split all the way up one side, and she was wearing boots. It was very difficult to describe. It was one of those "you have to see it to believe it" times.

I had an interesting conversation with a fellow from Tennessee. His wife was in the car. They were on their way home from the Northwest. He wanted a Kentucky bicycle map. We discussed the Land between the Lakes National Recreation Area and compared our Northwest trip to theirs, our trip was in 2002. He has not been in Alaska, North Dakota or Rhode Island, as I have been. But he has toured England and Scotland, as I have not. He checked on his family tree in Scotland, he said it has no branches. They took a cruise and visited a day each in Italy, Spain and France. I discussed Italy with him, having lived there for 3 years.

The same month, a couple from North Carolina was taking their three children out west. They had two weeks and would go as far as they could. They had traveled west about 10 years ago and wanted their children to experience as much of the US as they could. The children ranged in age from 5 or 6 to 9.

In July 2007 a man shared a different situation. He was married to his first wife and had a boy and a girl. They divorced; he married his second wife and had a boy and a girl. They too divorced. Now he's worked for first wife and her husband for several years. He has lived in their basement for several years. His second wife is now hiding out from her second husband---- and so it goes.

One day a man who was raised in Pembroke, close to Hopkinsville, came in with his son. He and his wife were visiting the son who lived in Hopkinsville. He and his wife now lived in Harlingen, Texas. I had visited an aunt and uncle who lived there; so we discussed that. This couple had lived in Marion, Kentucky for over 20 years. His wife had arthritis and took 5 pills a day for the pain. They had a nephew in the Dallas – Fort Worth area and had planned on moving there. Someone he met in Texas told him about Harlingen, they decided to move there. He said his wife is much better and down to 2 pills a day. The weather is better than the Dallas-Fort worth area, and he thanks the Lord for the man telling him about Harlingen.

Another sad story: A woman had macular-degeneration and was going blind. Her husband was trying to take her to see things and places that she wanted to go, while she still had her sight. She was a nice lady from Missouri. They were meeting their son in Alabama and were going to Florida to go on a cruise.

In March a little old lady with no teeth, and a different type of shoe on each foot, came in. She lived all over the states following the crops. She was in front of the Information center and asked permission to stay there long enough to rearrange her car. She had no money and said friends were going to send money to her. She was on her way to Wisconsin, and she asked about a soup kitchen. We supplied her lunch from the local Bank as they were doing a fund raiser that day. She came in three times; once to change into jeans and then twice to ask questions. Some ladies from Illinois commented on how full and junky her car was, especially on the dash. They were surprised the police had not stopped her because it was so piled up with stuff. She was probably there for about an hour. She was very difficult to understand.

A doctor was too frugal to pay for a campground. He first said that they just wanted to pull over to see the water. They had a large, old motorhome and wanted to camp by the water. I suggested the Marina to see the water but was not sure if they would be allowed to stay overnight. He used to practice in Marion, KY, some 40 years ago. They'd moved to California because his parents were ill and needed him. Now they live in Hopkinsville. He was a nice friendly guy; I think he had stopped in before with grandchildren getting information on the Land between the Lakes National Recreation Area. I surmised that his wife may not be well because of a remark he made and the fact that she never comes in.

I received another once in a lifetime request (remember the nude camping?). A couple from a city staying at the bed & breakfast in Cadiz wanted to experience the farm life. Or at least the husband did. He wanted to work a day on a farm to see what that life is like. But what he really wanted to do was milk a cow by hand. He said that he would settle for a goat but would rather it be a cow. The tourism director and I started making phone calls. One person's suggestion led to another and that led to a person who owns the last dairy farm in Calloway County, KY. This farm is about 35 to 40 miles to the west of Cadiz. This dairy farmer works with Murray State University students, showing them how a modern farm is operated. As chance would have it, he was expecting a group of students the Saturday that the city man was going to be in town. We arranged for him to join the student tour and he got his chance to milk a cow. We try to do our best for the visitors to our county!

Several years ago a couple from Independence, Missouri visited for quite a while. They were returning home from Chattanooga, Tennessee. They had been to see their daughter who was in a mental hospital there. They had hoped to bring her back to Missouri with them, but she had refused to go with her parents. They had taken her to several different doctors over the years and her medications had thus changed several times. They had brought her home from an institution about a year ago. The mother said that their daughter hadn't been very stable, but they had thought that with her medication she would be able to function normally enough. The daughter later borrowed their car to go buy hair coloring and a perm. She never returned and it took the better part of a year to find her. They said that their daughter was polar 2 schizophrenic, of which I know nothing. The mother said that they had really been through it over the last years with her. She didn't seem depressed, though. She really seemed to be handling the problems and was in good spirits.

I had a great conversation with a lady that had been a missionary in Africa for several years. She had always wanted to see Africa and decided after the death of her husband that then was the ideal time to go. Her children were grown, so she had no responsibilities toward them. She was 65 and very glad to be back. I told her about a lady that goes to our church that had been a missionary in Africa for several years.

A couple from Tennessee came in and visited quite a while. In this case, it was the man who did most of the talking. His wife was in and out of the building. Some locals had stopped in and they were interested in what he had to say. He'd had a boating accident several years before and had to have brain surgery. He said a song had come to him about being thankful for friends that had stood by him and helped him. He had been told that some people become violent after receiving this type of surgery; but he hadn't. I supposed that his wife had heard this story many times and had lived through it and that was why she didn't stay inside and join the conversation.

A woman spent quite a long time with me one day, back in 2001. She looked like she was in her mid-30's, but said she was born in 1959, which made her 42. She seemed childish, running around and talked very fast – a hyper type. She said that she spent her time hitchhiking all over the United States. She had recently spent time in Florida. In previous years she had been to California and New York. She cleaned buildings and homes and also waitressed. She would get rides from people and hand-outs from churches or other people. She told me that she had been raped twice. Once because she thought the man was taking her to clean his home. Her mother was deceased. An aunt she was fond of had also died, and her dad had remarried. He was almost 80 and had a heart condition. Her step-mother had said that she could live in their basement, but her father had said no. He didn't want any kids moving back into his house. They lived in the St. Louis, Missouri area.

One man spent a long time talking about his wife. He was sad and hurt. He could have written the "Somebody Did Somebody Wrong" song. They were from a small town a little west of here. She had wanted to go back to school. He had left their nice house to take a better paying job in Indiana. He was living in a one room place to save money to pay for her schooling. After all his sacrifices, she ended up leaving him for another man and he was crushed.

A man came in one spring to wait for a ride to take him home. He was here all afternoon before they picked him up. He said that he had been incarcerated for a few years. He said that he had not known about Jesus before prison. He'd had really long hair and a long beard before he had been imprisoned. He was now clean shaven and had short hair. He had very pretty eyes. He wasn't married, but he talked about his little boy. His son was 4 or 5 years old and had been born while he was in prison. He'd learned a lot about the Bible from the different preachers that had visited the prison. I've been going to church all of my life and have taken several different types of Bible studies. I don't even pretend to know or understand a lot of it, but I do know when people are way off base or saying things that are their opinion rather than actually from the Bible. He had so many plans; I wished him well. I hope he was able to avoid falling back in with former friends and getting into trouble again.

A couple came in to take a break from driving from Washington state to Knoxville, TN to visit family. The wife had met a woman from Missouri in an online support group for sufferers of cirrhosis of the liver, which they both had. She said that neither of them knew how or why they had contracted the disease. Through their online interactions, these ladies had become friends. Their husbands had secretly planned a meeting between the two women during this visit. The lady from Washington didn't know that she would soon meet her friend in person for the first time.

One October three nuns came into the Tourist Center after lunch. They were Dominican Sisters from Nashville on their way to St. Louis, Missouri. They were wearing long white habits with big sleeves. I always check the restrooms a few times a day to make sure that everything is OK. I found a long white envelope on top of the toilet paper dispenser with the word 'Mother' on it. I knew immediately it must belong to the sisters. I could feel money, credit cards and change in the envelope. I called Charles, the Tourism Director, and he said to open the envelope and see if there was any contact info of any kind in it. There was over $200 in cash and two gas cards with a name on them. When I closed at 5:00pm, I left a note on the door for the sisters to get in touch with me, hoping that they would return. I was concerned for them; no money, no gas card. I knew that if they could make it to St. Louis they would be taken care of. On Saturday, at my husband's suggestion, I called our local Catholic Church. Their answering machine message gave a contact phone number in Hopkinsville. I called that number and gave the priest the information and the name on the gas cards. He said that he would contact the appropriate people in Nashville. Sure enough, three of their sisters were at a conference in St. Louis. When the priest called me back, he was really enjoying this. Apparently, the envelope was left by a Mother Superior. The 'regular' nuns in Nashville had gotten a kick out of the fact that the Mother Superior would have chastised one of them for being so careless. The priest told me that the nuns "would get a lot of mileage out of this". The trio of sisters stopped on their way home on Sunday. I had left the envelope with the person working at the Tourist Center that day. The sisters asked for my address and I received a nice 'Thank You' note.

A couple from Florida came in and talked about how disappointed they had been. They had gone to a resort area near Denver, CO to attend their son's wedding. Once they got there, they drove all around the area looking for the wedding site. They saw campers and tents in different places, but apparently they didn't check them out. They ended up missing the wedding and the reception, which, they were told later, was like a luau, complete with a baked pig. They had ended up going to a local casino for the night and told me how nice the place had been. There was a lake or river in the back for fishing and a nice area to have a cookout. But still, all that way only to miss the wedding! They seemed really bummed out.

October 12, 2003

Dear Wanda,

The other two sisters and I stopped in Cadiz today at the Tourist Information Center where we had met you on Thursday. Sure enough, Mr. Calhoun had the envelope with our money and gas cards waiting for us. We were sorry we weren't able to see you again and say ***Thank You***. We were surely relieved to learn that you had found our lost items. It was very kind of you to arrange for someone to have them there for us on our return trip.

Even before we had realized that we had left our money there by mistake, we had remarked to one another about your kindness in taking time to welcome and talk with us on Thursday. The care you took to help us with our "lost" envelope was certainly more than kindness. It was Christian charity at its best. We are very grateful.

Our best way to say ***Thank You*** is always in prayer. We ask God to bless you for your goodness to us.

Sincerely,
Mother [illegible] and Sister

Thank you note received from the traveling nuns.

Several years ago, a very attractive woman shared her story with me. She had a daughter who was 15 years old and lived with her grandparents in Illinios. This lady's second husband was living in Nashville. Neither daughter nor husband would move. I can't begin to describe the agony this woman was going through. She and her husband had separated once. She was now driving back and forth, trying to be in both of their lives. Her husband was not at all understanding about how she felt about missing out on the important happenings and events in her daughter's life, or just being there for her.

I consider all our visitors special and try to meet their needs. There have been, however, a few that were better known than others. A few musicians, and other people with their bands, have stopped by to get directions. Probably the most well-known was Sarah Cannon, better known as Minnie Pearl. Another attendant was working that day, so I didn't get to meet her. She and her husband were on their way to Paducah, Kentucky. He waited in the car while she visited the ladies' room. She was very friendly.

One of the ladies from the TV station WPSD in Paducah, Kentucky, met her parents here. She had been one of my favorite people at that station. Her parents were very friendly. They were taking the granddaughter home with them while the "celebrity" and her husband went camping. I saw her again in Paducah at the Carson Center and she remembered me! Another time, one of WPSD's weathermen, and his family, stopped in. He was from the north and liked cold weather, yet they were moving out west.

Several stretch limousines have graced our parking lot, but I had no idea who the people were when they came in. I treat all alike.

In the 25 plus years that I've worked here, the part time people hired after me would visit from 2 to 4 hours to see how I would interact with the people. You learn to meet their needs. You wear a lot of hats. Be informative and friendly. Some wanted to get their information; find out where they made a wrong turn, get back on the right road and go. Others wanted to linger and visit. I like to make them feel like visitors in my home. They want to know all about the area. We encourage them to take

Business Rt. 68 if they're heading West, through the Land between the Lakes, instead of using the by-pass. Stretch out your information for people staying to include other surrounding counties. Talk about their state and places you've been. Keep the place clean and the brochure racks well stocked. Helping people is the main thing about working here at the welcome center. It makes you feel so good. There have been so many over the years really in need of gas, food or lodging.

Every act we commit, trivial or important, has its consequences. Like throwing a pebble into a pool and watching the ripples spread out farther, farther, far reaching. What we do, how we act and handle things, affects our children and grandchildren's lives.

People will comment on something we talked about a year or more before. They thanked me for some side trip I suggested. Sometimes notes were written to the director at the downtown Tourist Office.

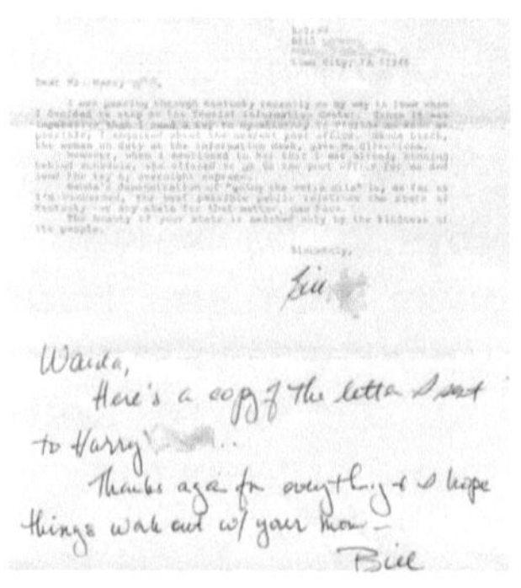

Wanda,
Here's a copy of the letter I sent to Harry ...
Thanks again for everything & I hope things work out w/ your mom —
Bill

A note sent to the Tourism Director.

The downtown Tourist Office closed three years ago and the Tourism Director has moved out to this office. Two years later the Tourist Center was renovated, adding two additional offices and was renamed the Commerce Center. After the renovations to the Commerce Center resulted in almost twice the space and a lot more glass to clean, we now have a person that comes in every two weeks to help clean. It's different now that people can come into the open, glassed-in, area and pick up the information that they need, when we are busy or the Commerce Center is closed. They can get brochures of the area 24/7. I still check with them to see if they are finding the information that they were looking for. Quite often they wait to talk or ask questions. Of course, a lot of people still come inside.

This is only a few of the memorable people I have met. So many times I was too busy to write down a few notes; of course you can only remember so much. It's not as colorful as it would have been if my husband had been able to add to, describe the people and weather conditions. As they used to say on Dragnet, years ago, "These are just the facts." I hope you have enjoyed reading about these characters as I have meeting them and trying to let you see them through my description.

Oh, and just for the record...... it's pronounced `kay-diz .

Memories and Impressions

By Wanda Lisch

There are so many beautiful things to see
As I stand in awe with humility.

The early blossoms of spring, the jonquils are out
The white, ghost-like pears and forsythias about.

We soon have redbuds, the dogwoods are in bloom
There are also the stars, and just look at that moon.

I watch the sunset, a rainbow, all the things God made
And mountains all colors – from white to a red shade.

A reflecting white cloud on a smooth as glass lake
Snowcapped mountains show up in the picture I take.

The rugged coast of Oregon, Tall evergreens out west
Hawaii, New England, can't decide which is best.

There are also the people, it takes all kind
They are all very different in body and mind.

The buildings range from historic to small
Some with stained glass windows and others so tall!

I've seen glaciers in Alaska, the Grand Tetons too
Old Faithful erupting and the San Diego Zoo.

I've climbed the leaning Tower of Pisa
Visited Naples, Venice and Rome

But always a place in my heart
Called Kentucky home.

Christmas At Golden Pond ....1940's

By Wanda Lisch

Over the hills to pick out the cedar tree
When I was young, my grampa and me.

He would point out a rabbit, I would mention the sky
We'd laugh and talk and the time flew by.

We rode in the wagon, he didn't own a car
No worry about gas, or a flat tire.

Mama baked cakes, always banana and jam
She would buy a fresh coconut, he supplied the ham.

The variety of candy made by Mimmie and Mother
The chicken and dressing, never so good by another.

The highlight of all our family meals
Was Mother's and Mimmie's 1930's tales.

Growing up in Kuttawa, all their friends and the fun
The hilarious stories of the pranks that were done.

The holidays aren't the same since they're all gone
Now they're spreading joy in their heavenly home.

Only the wind whispers fragments of stories past told
Only the hills and trees left of the memories we hold.

Miss Lizzie

By Wanda Lisch

Miss Lizzie was small, barely five feet tall
Tiny in weight, but she bossed them all.

Her grandsons from Michigan, loved to tease
They'd pull her apron strings, down to her knees.

She gave birth to five daughters, three lived to be grown
With a husband not well, she did it alone.

She worked very hard, from youth to middle age
By the time I knew her, she about had it made.

A house on the hill, overlooking the town
A yard with a slope, I loved to roll down.

She had a large garden, an orchard and animals galore
A milk cow, some chickens, ducks, geese and more.

She always gave to others, her food and her time
I can smell her coffee, on the stove in my mind.

I cherish her large bread bowl, it's wooden and worn
Always an apron over her dress she adorned.

She was my great-grandma, Elizabeth Adair Flora
She loved to visit us in Kuttawa, buy honey and more.

As the years past, she needed my grandmother Alice nearby
A move to Golden Pond in the mid 40's, my grandparents, Mother and I.

She built 2 new houses, down the road from each other
Then, in about ten years, she was called home to another.

This time her heavenly home when she was seventy-nine
This small feisty lady, this great-grandma of mine.

I'll always remember her strengths and her will
I'll always have fond memories of the house on the hill.

Forever Changed

Author Unknown

Can you see a change in me?
It may not be obvious to you.
I participate in family activities.
I attend reunions. I help plan holiday meals.

You tell me you're glad to see that I don't cry anymore.
But I do cry!
When everyone has gone – when it is safe – the tears fall.
I cry in privacy so my family won't worry.
I cry until I'm exhausted and finally sleep.

You tell me you admire my strength and my positive attitude.
But I am not strong.
I feel that I have lost control, and I panic when I think
about tomorrow, next week, next year. I go about the
routine of my job. I complete my assigned tasks.
I drink coffee and smile.

You tell me you're glad to see I'm over the death of my loved one.
But I'm not "over" it.
If I get over it, I would be the same as before my loved one died.
I will never be the same.
At times, I think I am going to heal,
But the pain of losing someone I loved so much
Has left a permanent scar on my heart.

You tell me you're so glad to see that I'm holding up so well.

But I am not holding up well.

Sometimes I want to lock the door and hide from the world. I spend time with my friends. I visit my neighbors. I appear calm and collected. I smile when appropriate.

You tell me it's good to see me back to my "old self".

But I will never be back to my "old self".

Death and grief have touched my life.

But I am forever changed!

Acknowledgements

There are several people I extend my appreciation to for their help. I thought, after Bill's death, that this was a lost dream.

Several years ago, **Frank Weer** had suggested the title when he and his wife, Nell, were having lunch with Bill and me.

Thanks to:

Gloria Hobbs Traville was a classmate of Bill's from Collinsville, Illinois, who now lives in Kansas. She encouraged me about a year after Bill's death, when I had given up on this idea.

Betty Simonson, for the many hours we struggled over old notes. She typed while I deciphered the handwritten pages.

LeKida Hughes also did typing for me. By this time I had gotten my notes into legible handwriting.

Dan Whitehouse took those stories and organized them into similar situations and sections of the world. This couldn't have been done without him.

Glenn McGill, for making many helpful suggestions.

Betsy Taylor and **Martha Maxfield**, for proofreading the many drafts we went through.

Drew Hudgins at Hudge Media, LLC, help and suggestions with the dust jacket design.

And all the rest of my family and friends, for all your encouragement.

About the Author

Wanda Lisch was born in Kuttawa, KY. Her parents, Dickie and Pauline Wilferd, were divorced by the time she was 4 years old. She and her mother then moved to Golden Pond, KY. A few years later, her mother remarried and Wanda grew up with a step-brother, Ray. After graduating high school Wanda married Ed McGill. They had two children; Eddie, born in 1960, and Chris Michele, born in 1969.

Wanda's husband was in the military which meant that the family moved often, as is often the case with military families. While they were stationed in Italy for three years the family visited Germany, Austria, Switzerland, The Netherlands and much of Italy. Once back in the U.S. they lived in New Mexico, Virginia, Maryland, North Carolina, Massachusetts and Hawaii, among other places.

Wanda and Ed divorced in 1982. She married Bill Lisch in 1984. Wanda and Bill enjoyed traveling together but always looked forward to returning home to family and friends.

Wanda has enjoyed working at the Cadiz-Trigg County Tourist Information Center for more than 25 years. Her years involved in the military life and meeting people from all over the world has prepared her to deal with the many situations at the Tourist Center.

All kinds of questions are asked of her and strangers tell her stories about their lives. Some of those stories are what makes up this book.

www.ingramcontent.com/pod-product-compliance
Ingram Content Group UK Ltd.
Pitfield, Milton Keynes, MK11 3LW, UK
UKHW040559210726
13854UKWH00008B/1499